IF YOU KNEW

INSPIRATIONAL QUOTES AND QUESTIONS
TO LIBERATE THE MIND AND HEAL THE HEART

DEBORAH   SAUNDERS

Published June 2020.

ISBN: 9798646615375

APPROBATIONS

This book seems to ask simple questions, but the results will be amazingly profound. The subtitle is true: Questions to liberate the mind and heal the heart. This is exactly what this book aims to do – to help people think outside of the box that was created for them in childhood, to challenge their limiting beliefs and find their own, individual truth.

Dr Miriam Adahan PHD, best selling author and clinical psychotherapist

---

Deborah Saunders has done the world a valuable service with her latest publication, If You Knew...which can enable readers to see their challenges and struggles in a fresh new light of hope. At the end of the day, it is not our challenges which control our lives but how we look at and deal with them which makes all the difference.

Dr Meir Wikler, psychotherapist, author and international speaker

INTRODUCTION

I was once talking to Michelle, an enthusiastic member of one of my personal-development groups. Smiling, she told me that she had seen my recently published book *Being & Becoming.* "Next," she said, "we need a book of 'one-liners' which we can pick up in our vulnerable moments to help us get our stability and empowerment back."

It was an interesting thought, and although I was not sure exactly what this book would look like and which format it would have, I knew that it would come.

You are holding the result in your hand.

Each of us has a deep knowledge of truth inside ourselves. We recognize this truth when we come across it. It feels familiar and comfortable. We *know* it is correct. Some people say, "It just clicked"; some people say, "It was a gut feeling"; some people don't say anything — they just sense an inner knowing. All are experiencing their deep inner knowledge.

As we go through life, we pick up assumptions about ourselves, life, and others that block this inner clarity, and we can begin to live life as if these foreign assumptions are accurate representations of the facts. In my work as a therapist, I come across these individual assumptions that can create a block to the inner knowledge and clear direction to the people who have them. In this book, I present common assumptions that I have encountered.

I discovered a powerful way to turn these assumptions around in a manner that helps us connect to our deep knowledge of truth which, when accessed, can clear our minds of unhelpful, disempowering thoughts and reconnect us with our inner flow of clarity and empowerment.[1] We then encounter our potential for opportunity, trust, acceptance, connection, and resilience toward the life circumstances that we face.

I call this method "going around the back door of our limiting assumptions." Instead of meeting our limiting assumptions head-on and getting into a debate with them, we do not even need to engage them. We can choose to leave them be and introduce liberating beliefs which will engage us and lead us to an internal feeling of empowerment and self-worth.

Allow me to explain this concept with an example:

Dinah was struggling in her family relationships and wanted to enjoy them more. We determined that her limiting assumption was that she felt she was undeserving of love. The question that we constructed for her was, "If you knew that you were deserving of love, how would you feel in your relationships?" Her face relaxed as she suddenly felt liberated from the limiting belief. Her emotional shift was visible.

I was amazed at how quickly she was able to access her inner healthy core of knowledge that

---

1. Nancy Kline, *Time to Think* (Octopus Books, 1998).

she is deserving of love. With this question, she connected to it. She "went around the back door" instead of arguing with the completely irrational assumption that she is unworthy of love. When the new, empowering knowledge came through, she automatically connected to it without a fight.

I am privileged in my job as a therapist to help people access their inner well-being. This book is a compilation of many of the questions that have proved helpful in mapping the way for people to access their inner calm, clarity, and confidence. We all have the same spiritual core, however, we all have different assumptions that distract us from living with this well-being. I have tried, as much as possible, to include a variety of different beliefs that people get stuck on so that this book can be helpful to a wide range of people. Additionally, we may need to uproot different assumptions at different stages of our lives, so keep reading this book whenever you feel the need to!

HOW TO USE THIS BOOK

If you will, *If You Knew* is like a menu of questions that have the potential to help you shift in a positive way. Your job is to choose what you want from the menu. Some of the questions have specific, concrete answers, however, their main power is experiential — triggering an emotional space within you that will give you a different perspective. I imagine it like a beautiful garden with a lock on the gate. These questions unlock the gate and free you from your previous limiting beliefs, giving you the opportunity to experience life in a much more empowered and expansive way. Once you are in the "garden," life looks clearer, and solutions are accessed more easily.

Essentially, all these questions tackle the same two limiting assumptions: "I am not good enough" and "I cannot trust myself." These foundational misconceptions then evolve into many different "flavors" of assumptions which the questions in this book address. Because of these two main themes of self-acceptance and self-trust, there is some repetition in the different sections of similar questions. This is done with intent, as they are relevant in a variety of contexts.

As you will see, there are different categories in this book. Everyone has different struggles, so I want to make it easier for people to zone in and focus on the areas that are a challenge for them.

I have put the subjects in alphabetical order for ease of reference.

My sincere hope is that *If You Knew* will generate your inner peace and empowerment in a way that benefits you in your life.

Deborah Saunders

CONTENTS

You may feel like you are stuck in the feeling of anxiety forever and cannot imagine feeling better.

If you knew that the anxiety will pass, how would you feel?

You may judge yourself harshly for feeling anxious and feel silly about it.

If you knew that you can give yourself compassion and respect while you feel anxious, how would you feel?

You may feel like you have failed because you feel anxious.

If you knew that anxiety is a challenge, not a failure, what would this knowledge give you?

You may feel like your dignity, worthiness, and value diminish when you feel anxious.

If you knew that you are still a dignified, worthy, and valuable person while you feel anxious, what would this knowledge give you?

You may feel the need to try to control the past, the future, or others, which leads to anxiety.

If you knew that you can give yourself permission to let go of controlling the past, the future, or other people, how would you feel?

You may lose sight of your potential to have healthy thoughts about the same life circumstances that you feel anxious about.

If you knew that you have the capacity to have calm, clear thoughts about the same life circumstances, how would you feel?

You may forget that you will not always feel this tense.

If you knew that when you are tense you can trust that you will relax again, what would this realization give you?

Accepting the anxiety as a challenge rather than a failure, helping ourselves through it rather than fighting it, letting go of trying to control things that are not in our control, and easing back into the liberating truth that the healing comes directly from God and we just need to take helpful steps of self-care (including seeking professional help when necessary) are all effective tools for tuning into our inner well-being in the face of anxiety.

COMPARING TO OTHERS

Be yourself; everyone else is already taken![2]

A flower does not think of competing with the flower next to it; it just blooms.

You may think the grass is greener on the other side, but if you take the time to water your own grass, you may realize it is just as green.

2. Oscar Wilde.

Have you ever looked at other people's achievements or capabilities and felt inferior or inadequate compared to them? They seemed more competent, more important, and more capable than you. It is not a pleasant experience! The more we focus on the other person, the less confident we feel about ourselves.

You may feel insignificant and not as valuable as others.

If you knew that you are important and valuable in your own right, how would you feel?

———— • ————

You may only see your limitations and other people's strengths. You may forget your right to have your own blend of strengths and limitations.

If you knew that everyone has his or her own, unique blend of strengths and limitations, how would you feel?

———— • ————

You may feel that this insecurity represents you rather than mirroring an insecure space you have gone into.

If you knew that insecurity comes from your mind, not from the reality of who you are, what would this understanding give you?

You may feel like you have a raw deal compared to others around you.

If you knew that everything you have is perfect for you, what would this realization change for you?

You may overlook the fact that by comparing yourself to others you are unintentionally holding yourself back from utilizing your ability to feel confident.

If you knew that you could give yourself permission to be confident in yourself, how would you feel?

The more comfortable we are with the package of who we are, the less we feel the need to compare ourselves to others. We stop measuring ourselves against others and finding ourselves inferior or superior to them and instead discover an equality and a respect of ourselves and others. We look at others and learn from them, but in no way does this threaten or unsettle us.

CHOICES

The only way we can change the world is by taking responsibility for our part in it.

May your choices reflect your hopes, not your fears.[3]

You cannot go back and change the beginning, but you can start where you are and change the ending.[4]

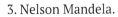

3. Nelson Mandela.
4. C. S. Lewis.

Life happens. We face challenges, people act in certain ways, and situations happen around us. Sometimes we may feel like we are victims, like things just happen to us and we have no control.

You may feel trapped into reacting to what is going on around you.

If you knew that you are always free to choose how you respond to what goes on around you, what would you do differently?

———— ● ————

You may focus your energy on others' choices and feel unmotivated with regard to your own choices.

If you knew that you can only control your own choices and can let go of the choices of others, how would you feel?

———— ● ————

You may feel trapped in the choices of previous moments.

If you knew that each moment presents a new opportunity for choice, what would this knowledge open up for you?

———————— ● ————————

The secret to control is in our choices. We do not have control over what comes *at* us; we have control over what comes *from* us. Our strength lies in our responses, our choices, our learning, and our triumphs.

FEAR

Courage is not the absence of fear, but the triumph over it.[5]

Our deepest fear is not that we are inadequate. Our deepest fear is that we are powerful beyond measure.[6]

Don't be pushed around by the fears in your mind; be led by the dreams in your heart.[7]

---

5. Nelson Mandela.
6. *Ibid*.
7. Roy T. Bennett.

We all have fears, however, we tend to feel alone in our fear. We may judge ourselves as weak or silly and tell ourselves to "snap out of it," which does not work. More often than not, the fear does not match the reality, but it still pumps through us and feels real to us. It may cause our minds to race.

You may feel threatened by your fear and try to fight it.

If you knew that you can accept your fear without needing to escape it, what would that give you?

———————— ● ————————

When you are experiencing fear, it may feel all-encompassing.

If you knew that even in a moment of fear there is a space inside you that is completely calm, trusting, and free of fear, how would you feel?

———————— ● ————————

When you are experiencing fear you may feel alone and that you are the only one who has fears.

If you knew that everyone has fears, albeit about different things, what would that knowledge give you?

———————— ● ————————

You may find yourself panicking in the face of the unknown.

If you knew that you have the capacity to be comfortable with the unknown, how would you feel?

———————— ● ————————

You may feel that your fears or external circumstances can threaten your inner peace.

If you knew that you always have inner security which cannot be swayed by anything, how would you feel?

———————— ● ————————

When we are able to accept our fears without judging ourselves for them, this frees up our energy to reassure ourselves and face the fear with dignity and confidence rather than feeling the need to run away from it. We trust our resilience, the God-given strength within us, to deal with life despite our fear.

GUILT

No amount of guilt can change the past, and no amount of worry can change the future.

Your mistakes do not define you.

Let go of the guilt; keep hold of the lessons.

Many of us can relate to the sinking feeling of guilt when we feel an uncomfortable urgency and a lack of ability to feel our worthiness or freedom in the moment. Sometimes we know that the guilt is irrational, but we still feel it. We may feel guilty when other people around us are struggling. This form of guilt is hinged on an expectation of ourselves to control all aspects of life perfectly. We blame ourselves for not being able to.

You may feel that your guilt is justified and that you need to feel negatively about yourself.

If you knew that you do not need to take disempowering guilt seriously, how would you feel?

———— ● ————

You may feel that because of your mistakes you have to relinquish your right to be valued and loved.

If you knew that you are valuable and lovable despite your failures, what would this insight give you?

You may think it is weak to admit that you have done something wrong.

If you knew that it is courageous to admit our mistakes, what would that change?

———————— ● ————————

You may think that letting go of guilt means you don't care about your failures.

If you knew that letting go of guilt does not mean you don't care, it means you want to move forward, how would that change things for you?

———————— ● ————————

You may feel that if you face up to what you have done wrong, you have to give up on yourself.

If you knew that facing up to your wrongdoings allows you to make amends and learn from past failures, how would you feel?

———————— ● ————————

You may not realize that you are holding your mistakes or limitations against yourself. You may not realize that you can allow yourself to forgive yourself.

If you knew that you can forgive yourself for your mistakes, how would you see things differently?

———————— ● ————————

Sometimes, our path through guilt into empowerment is forgiving ourselves for our mistakes and failures. It is about connecting to ourselves beyond the mistakes and tuning back into our unconditional worth. Then we are in a position to reflect on things and make amends or learn from our failures. Sometimes, when the guilt is irrational, it is about letting go of our expectation to be perfect and control past events or other people.

We can reacquire our empowerment.
It is ours.

LETTING GO OF THE PAST

Those mountains that you are carrying, you were only supposed to climb.

Never be a prisoner of your past. It was just a lesson, not a life sentence.

Forgiveness is giving up on the hope of a different past.[8]

---

8. Oprah Winfrey.

We sometimes feel stuck because of past events. We feel disempowered, resentful of those involved in the events, and a lack of drive to move forward. We may feel that past situations or memories sap some of our strength. Life may feel heavy and difficult.

You may feel stuck because of past life circumstances.

If you knew that the only place you are imprisoned by the past is in your own mind, what would that open up for you?

———— ● ————

You may doubt that you have the freedom and empowerment to move forward.

If you knew that you are never stuck and that there is always the opportunity to move forward, what would this knowledge give you?

———— ● ————

You may doubt that you can think differently with regard to the areas of your life that you would like to.

If you knew that you have the capacity to let go of old, unhelpful thought patterns, how would you feel?

———————— ● ————————

You may feel stuck in past failures and feel unable to move past them.

If you knew that you can let go of past failures and move forward in the way that you want to, how would you feel?

———————— ● ————————

You may feel like moving forward from past trauma and difficulties undermines what you have been through.

If you knew that letting go of past traumas and difficulties is a gift to yourself, alongside a genuine acknowledgment of past pain, how would you feel?

———————— ● ————————

When we realize that the ability to move forward is always within our grasp, and while we can and should give ourselves the necessary support to heal, we can choose to do so in the here and now, we are never stuck or at the mercy of others. We can choose to let go of making ourselves victims. We can choose to learn from the past, and we can choose to remember that this is a strong and powerful move.

MARRIAGE

Marriage is not a noun, it is a verb
. . . It is not something you get, it is
something you do. It is the way you
give to your spouse every day.[9]

I can't promise to fix all your
problems, but I promise you
won't face them alone.

9. Barbara De Angelis.

Do you ever feel stuck in your marriage?

Do you wonder where your connection to your spouse has gone and what you can do to retrieve it?

Do you get disempowered by your spouse's moods, issues, or choices?

You may feel alone in your marriage if you are struggling to connect to your spouse or in any other aspect of your marriage.

If you knew that God is the third partner in your marriage, how would you feel?

———————— ● ————————

You may feel frustrated or distracted by your spouse's issues or poor life choices and unmotivated to focus on your issues or choices.

If you knew that you do not need to take responsibility for your spouse's actions, only your own, how would you feel?

You may feel disillusioned when you lose the feeling of connection to your spouse. In that moment, you may panic that your marriage is not secure.

If you knew that the ups and downs of marriage do not alter your deep, real connection with your spouse, how would you feel?

You may feel stuck because of the times when you have acted wrongly toward your spouse and feel disempowered as a result.

If you knew that you can forgive yourself for your mistakes in your marriage and move forward by learning from them, how would you feel?

You may doubt whether you have the capacity and resources to be a good spouse.

If you knew that you can trust yourself to have the resources to give to your spouse in the way that he or she deserves, how would you feel?

You may feel like trusting yourself in your marriage means you have to do it on your own without support.

If you knew that you can reach out for support when necessary to give you clarity and empowerment in your marriage, what action would you take?

———————— ● ————————

You may get stuck in your spouse's moods and feel dependent on him or her for your own well-being. You may feel over-responsible for your spouse's mood and well-being.

If you knew that you and your spouse each have your own, independent source of well-being for you to utilize in life and in your marriage, how would you feel?

———————— ● ————————

A healthy marriage is one in which two people with their own identities and blends of strengths, weaknesses, vulnerability, and wisdom connect and share to create something so much more powerful that an individual can alone. There must be healthy dependency in which each is a respected person in his or her own right and has a sense of self to then contribute to the marriage.

MOODS AND EMOTIONS

There is nothing as whole
as a broken heart.[10]

However strong your emotions
are, you are still you.

We cannot control the wind,
but we can adjust our sails.[11]

A little bit of light pushes
away a lot of darkness.[12]

---

10. Rabbi of Kotsk.
11. Jewish Proverb.
12. *ibid*.

As human beings we all experience the ups and downs of emotions and moods. It can sometimes feel a little like a roller-coaster ride, and as much as we try, we cannot get off!

You may feel yourself judging or resisting your feelings.

If you knew that it is OK to relax and accept whatever you feel, what would change for you?

———— • ————

You may feel that accepting your feelings means you are going to lose control and act on them.

If you knew that accepting your feelings does not necessarily mean acting on them, what would this clarity give you?

———— • ————

You may feel that you are weak when you experience insecurity or uncomfortable emotions.

If you knew that you are still strong even when you feel insecure, how would you see your moods differently?

·

You may feel threatened by unhelpful thoughts that pass through you mind and unsure how to deal with them.

If you knew that you do not need to take unhelpful thinking seriously and that you can let it pass, how would you feel?

·

You may forget that however intense your moods or emotions are, your inner core is always healthy.

If you knew that you are anchored in resilience, security, and strength, how would you feel?

·

You may feel that your moods and emotions are wreaking havoc on all levels and forget your deep inner confidence and calm.

If you knew that you have a stream of confidence and calm constantly flowing through you, how would you feel?

———————— • ————————

You may feel that your difficult moods and emotions will last forever, and you cannot imagine feeling better.

If you knew that you could trust that your difficult moods and emotions will pass, how would you view them differently?

———————— • ————————

You may feel confused and conflicted by strong emotions that pull in a completely different direction from what you know innately to be true.

If you knew that it is OK to feel one thing while knowing that something else is true, what would you realize?

———————— • ————————

When we understand that our moods and emotions are what we experience but not who we are, although we still feel them, we do not get as lost in them or feel so threatened by them. They no longer become our identity, but something that we pass through, like a plane passing through turbulence. It does not weaken the plane; it is something that the plane goes through. We always remain our resilient selves, before, during, and after we experience moods and emotions.

OVER-RESPONSIBILITY

Don't let other people's irresponsibility become your responsibility.

Sometimes we give so much [to others] that we end up losing ourselves.

It is not our job to fix people. It is our job to love them even while they are broken.

Do you find yourself constantly thinking and worrying about others in a way that saps your energy or calm?

Do you feel an urgency to rescue others from their difficulties and guilt when you are unable to?

Do you find that you neglect your self-care in the process of caring for others?

We all have responsibilities toward ourselves and others. Responsibility is not heavy; feeling the need to control is. When we step out of the arena of our own specific responsibility into the arena of trying to control others, we feel heaviness. This is what over-responsibility is.

You may feel that your value is intertwined with how well you are giving to others.

If you knew that your value is totally independent of how well you give to others, how would you feel?

You may feel responsible for others and feel heavy and pulled in all directions as a result.

If you knew that you are only responsible to fulfill your duty in life, what would you let go of?

———— ● ————

You may feel a pull to control the decisions, struggles, or moods of others.

If you knew that you cannot control anyone but yourself, what would you let go of?

———— ● ————

You may find yourself neglecting your self-care in the process of focusing too much on helping others.

If you knew that you have the ability to balance caring for yourself and caring for others, what would you do differently?

———— ● ————

You may feel that it is your responsibility to rescue others rather than clarifying your role in giving to them and doing that to the best of your ability.

If you knew that you could give yourself permission to let go of responsibility *for* other people and focus on any role you have *toward* them, how would you feel?

———— ● ————

You may feel that you need to deal with others' lives on their behalf rather than supporting them in dealing with their lives.

If you knew that you only need to give to others, not deal with life for them, how would you feel in your relationships?

———— ● ————

You may feel an urgency to help others and that if you do not help them (even if it is obviously wrong for you), they will not get the help that they need.

If you knew that God is the only One who can rescue people, how would you feel?

You may feel that not rescuing others from their difficulties means that you do not care about them.

If you knew that letting go of responsibility for others does not mean you are letting go of caring about them, what would this knowledge give you?

———————— ● ————————

You may disregard or be unaware of your own feelings and thoughts regarding the struggles of those around you instead of giving them space and acceptance.

If you knew that you have a right to have your own feelings and thoughts about the struggles of those around you, how would you feel?

———————— ● ————————

Over-responsibility is when we stop focusing on responsibility *toward* others and feel responsibility *for* others. Stepping back into what is really ours to deal with and letting go of the rest allows us to feel empowered and care for others competently, rather than disempowered and out of our depth.

OVERWHELM

What lies behind us and what
lies before us are little matters
compared to what lies within us.[13]

The power behind me is greater
than the problem in front of me.

Faith is taking the first step
even when you cannot see
the whole staircase.[14]

13. Ralph Waldo Emerson.
14. Martin Luther King.

We all have times when what we have to deal with seems huge, and we feel incompetent and disempowered. We may start to feel stressed, tense, alone, or resentful toward the people around us.

You may feel tension and pressure when planning or working toward events.

If you knew that it is your job to put in effort but the results are on God's shoulders, how would you feel about upcoming events or situations?

———— ● ————

You may try to multitask and feel stressed or rushed.

If you knew that all you need to focus on right now is your next right action, what would you do?

———— ● ————

You may doubt that you have been given the resources you need.

If you knew that God is giving you all the resources you need to deal with what you have to in each moment, how would you feel?

You may feel that your stress is overtaking you.

If you knew that right now, beneath your tension is a calm space within you, what would this knowledge give you?

You may judge overwhelm and stress as a failure rather than a normal part of life.

If you knew that it is OK to be overwhelmed and stressed at times, what would this insight give you?

You might doubt your competence in dealing with all the things you need to.

If you knew that you could trust yourself to do what you need to, how would you feel?

———— ● ————

You may feel threatened by stress instead of accepting its message to slow down internally.

If you knew that stress is merely an "alarm bell" to let you know that your mind has sped up, how would you feel?

———— ● ————

When we are able to accept whatever we are feeling and then ground ourselves in trust that we have the resources to deal with what we need to in life, letting go of trying to control everything and knowing that we can delegate appropriately to others, we step back into the strength that God is giving us to deal with what we have to in the moment and leave everything else in His hands.

PARENTING

Are you the adult you want
your child to become?[15]

Children are not a distraction
from important work; they
are the important work.[16]

Deal with your children the way
you would want to be dealt with.

Don't rescue your child
from a challenge. Teach
them how to face it.

Treat a child as though he is the
person he is capable of becoming.[17]

---

15. Brene Brown.
16. C. S. Lewis.
17. Haim Ginot.

As parents we may feel many different emotions such as guilt, worry, overwhelm, fear, insecurity, and uncertainty. We may feel constantly pulled by the demands of our children and lose our sense of being grounded. We can feel confused about how to handle our parenting challenges and situations that our children are facing.

You may sometimes doubt your ability to parent well.

If you knew that you are being imbued (by God) with all the necessary resources to parent your children, how would you feel?

———————— ● ————————

You may feel pressure to be a perfect parent and not allow yourself or your child to have ups and downs.

If you knew that it is OK to have ups and downs in parenting, how would you feel?

———————— ● ————————

You may get distracted sometimes and focus on your child's choices instead of empowering your own choices as a parent in relation to your child's behavior.

If you knew that you cannot control your child's choices, only your own, what would you let go of?

———— ● ————

You may forget to respect your child's ability to take responsibility for the consequences of their actions and instead rescue them or criticize them.

If you knew that you can trust your child to take age-appropriate responsibility for their actions, what would that change?

———— ● ————

You may focus too much on your child's behavior and forget that a huge factor in parenting is how you, as a parent, model appropriate behavior.

If you knew that the greatest lessons to your children are how you act, what would you keep doing or do differently?

You may rescue your child from their own feelings by placating them too quickly. You may rescue your child from challenges that could help them grow instead of giving them support to deal with those challenges.

If you knew that your child has a right to have their own feelings and challenges, what would that change? How would you support your child rather than rescuing them?

———————— ● ————————

You may feel threatened and trapped by your child's behavior.

If you knew that no matter how your child behaves, you are never a victim of his choices and are always able to choose your reaction, how would you feel?

———————— ● ————————

You may feel dependent on your child's good mood or how well they are doing to feel OK.

If you knew that you have your own source of well-being, independent of how your child is doing, how would you feel?

———————— ● ————————

You may feel that your child is totally dependent on you for their well-being instead of trusting that they have their own source of well-being.

If you knew that your child has their own source of well-being, independent of you, how would you feel?

———————— ● ————————

You may feel overwhelmed by the responsibility you have as your child's parent.

If you knew that you need to take responsible action as a parent, however, the results are in God's hands, how would you feel?

———————— ● ————————

You may feel trapped and heavy due to your mistakes and limitations as a parent.

If you knew that you can forgive yourself for your parenting mistakes and vulnerabilities, how would you feel?

———————— • ————————

It is important to periodically gain clarity of our role as our children's parents, trust in the God-given resources we have to fulfill this role, and recognize that we need to take responsible action as parents and do the best we can, knowing that the results come from God. We can aim to strike the balance between investing in our children, ensuring that their needs are met, and then stepping back into the ease and knowledge that God is taking care of them and pumping them with the resources they need for their life's journey.

PEOPLE PLEASING

The more you love your decisions, the less you need others to love them.

You owe yourself the love that you so freely give to others.

Don't base your self-worth on what other people think of you.

People will treat you the way you allow them to.

We can sometimes find ourselves making decisions, saying things, or acting in certain ways, and if we are honest we will realize that these behaviors are not stemming from what we feel is right, from what we are choosing for ourselves; rather, they are triggered by a need for approval by others. In a way, we feel that we are waiting for permission from another person to feel OK about ourselves. We inadvertently throw the control outside ourselves instead of committing to value ourselves and allow ourselves to make healthy decisions.

You may feel that you cannot manage if someone disapproves of you.

If you knew that you have the capacity to deal with disapproval from others, how would you feel?

You may feel that you have no choice but to say yes to the demands or requests of others.

If you knew that you have a right to say no, when appropriate, to the demands or requests of others, how would you feel?

———— ● ————

You may disregard your own right to receive care and compassion and only direct these traits toward thers.

If you knew that you are worthy of care and compassion, what would you do differently?

———— ● ————

You may undermine your own importance.

If you knew that you are important, how would you see yourself?

———— ● ————

You may feel a drive to prove that you are worthy by gaining the approval of others.

If you knew that you are worthy as you are and do not need to prove it, how would you feel?

———————— ● ————————

The trick is to be honest with ourselves when pleasing others. If we are doing it to *give*, it is a powerful spiritual act. If we are doing it to *gain approval*, it stems from fear and tends to end in resentment and insecurity. Let us take back our autonomy and please people when it is appropriate and confidently and sensitively make effective decisions, even at the risk of disapproval.

PERFECTIONISM

The greatest mistake a person can make is to be afraid of making one.[18]

I never lose; I either win or learn.[19]

The greatest glory in living is not by never falling, it is by rising each time we fall.[20]

18. Elbert Hubbard.
19. Nelson Mandela.
20. *ibid*.

Perfectionism is when we get stuck in the assumption that if we want to be able to value ourselves, we have to be perfect. This creates a desperate drive to achieve perfection as if our life depends on it. On some level we believe that it does! We feel a constant fear of failure and are very hard on ourselves, constantly pushing ourselves to keep moving forward with no allowance for ups, downs, limitations, or vulnerability.

You may feel that you are never allowed to make mistakes.

If you knew that it is OK to make mistakes, how would you feel?

———————— ● ————————

You may feel that your value diminishes when you make mistakes. You may feel like giving up.

If you knew that you are valuable even when you make mistakes, how would you feel? What action would you take?

———————— ● ————————

You may feel ashamed of your imperfections.

If you knew that you can embrace your imperfections, how would you feel?

———————— ● ————————

You may feel pressure to be perfect in order to prove your worth.

If you knew that you are constantly lovable, worthy, and valuable, irrespective of your performance, how would you feel?

———————— ● ————————

You may feel that life has to look like a perfect upward line with no downs.

If you knew that it is OK to have ups and downs, how would you feel?

———————— ● ————————

Optimalism[21] is the healthy alternative to perfectionism: we are aiming high, however, we are traveling on the solid ground of being valuable because of who we are, not because of how we are performing. This allows us to have ups and downs, make mistakes, accept our limitations and vulnerabilities, and enjoy a journey of growth and discovery rather than trying to force ourselves along a straight and rigid path of life.

21. Tal Ben Shachar introduces this word in his book *The Pursuit of Perfect* (McGraw-Hill 2000).

POWER STRUGGLES

People who want power will always try to control those who truly have it.[22]

The most common way people give up their power is by thinking that they do not have any.[23]

Humility is not thinking less of yourself, it is thinking of yourself less.[24]

----

22. Prairie Johnson.
23. Alice Walker.
24. Rick Warren.

Sometimes, due to our limiting assumptions, we may surrender some of our power to another person and begin to feel inferior to them and allow them to have unhealthy control over us. We may feel that we have no choice but to go along with what they want. Alternatively, sometimes we forget that other people are entitled to their power and we undermine their rights and equality, causing us to feel superior. We stop respecting their right to have an opinion or preference.

You may be blind to your own power and value or blind to that of others.

If you knew that every person was created by God with power and value, how would this knowledge affect your life?

You may feel that you are powerless in the face of certain people, forgetting that you are inadvertently allowing yourself to be controlled.

If you knew that no one has the ability to control you, what would this knowledge give you?

───────── ◉ ─────────

You may feel coerced into acting a certain way and that you are not in control of your own choices in relation to the behavior of others.

If you knew that you have the right to make your own choices regardless of how other people behave, what would you do differently?

───────── ◉ ─────────

You may forget that you have a right to be respected.

If you knew that you have a right to have your own opinions and preferences which deserve to be respected (although this may not always actually happen), how would you feel?

In reality, we are receiving 100 percent power from God in every moment. When we tune into reality, we see that there can be respect for both our rights and individuality and the rights and individuality of others.

RELATIONSHIPS

The world is a mirror that reflects
the way you feel about yourself.[25]

Serenity is not the absence
of conflict but the ability
to cope with it.[26]

25. Lazer Brody.
26. 12-Step Program.

When we struggle with relationships, we may feel that they are beyond our control. We may have the misconception that we are victims of the other person. We sometimes despair of change, though we desperately want it. It feels like it is out of our reach.

You may feel disempowered in your relationships, forgetting that you have ultimate control over your choices.

If you knew that you are never a victim of another person, but always have the freedom to choose how to react, what would that change?

———— ● ————

You may feel stuck in the dysfunctional patterns of relationships in your life.

If you knew that you have the power to make positive changes in your relationships, what action would you take?

———— ● ————

You may forget your right to receive respect from others and begin to tolerate inappropriate behavior, or you may behave inappropriately toward others, overlooking their right for respect.

If you knew that you have a right to be respected and a duty to respect others, how would that affect your relationships?

You may feel that until the other person changes, you are stuck in this struggle.

If you knew that your experience of another person comes from your mind and you have the potential to shift to a more empowered mind-set in the face of the same behavior, how would you see things differently?

You may feel out of your depth with regard to what you are dealing with in certain relationships and forget that it is a strong move to reach out for the right support.

If you knew that you can reach out for support if you need it, what would you do?

———————— • ————————

Realizing that our struggle in relationships has everything to do with ourselves — not in a way of blame, but in a way of freedom to choose how to go forward — is very empowering. Our appreciation of our worth and the worth of others, commitment to respecting ourselves and others, and ability to reach out for appropriate support come from the inside, radiating outward with the potential to transform our relationships.

We can trust that God is a partner in our relationships, and if we reach out, we will be helped to navigate them in a good direction.

RESENTMENT

As I walked to the gate that
would lead me to my freedom,
I knew that if I did not leave my
bitterness and anger behind,
I would still be in prison.[27]

Forgiveness doesn't excuse their
behavior. Forgiveness prevents their
behavior from destroying your heart.

Holding a grudge doesn't make
you strong, it makes you bitter.
Forgiveness doesn't make you
weak, it sets you free.[28]

27. Nelson Mandela.
28. Dave Willis.

Do you tense up when you think about a particular person or he or she is mentioned in a conversation?

Do you feel heavy, frustrated feelings toward others?

Thinking about it, do you feel less powerful than those you resent?

Resentment is disempowering. We feel like victims, stuck with nowhere to move. We are resentful when we feel out of control and have seemingly lost the power to make choices and have an independent response to life events. We feel trapped by others and inadvertently surrender our power to them.

You may think that forgiveness is for the benefit of the person you are forgiving.

If you knew that forgiveness is a gift to yourself that sets you free, what would that change for you?

You may think that forgiveness means you need to reconnect to the other person.

If you knew that forgiveness may or may not mean reconciliation, since some people are not safe or healthy to interact with, how would you go forward?

———————— ● ————————

You may forget your right to create boundaries in your relationships.

If you knew that you have a right to create healthy boundaries with regard to how to interact with the person in the future, what would you commit to?

———————— ● ————————

You may think that forgiveness condones the wrong act.

If you knew that forgiveness merely moves the wrongdoing off of your heart and places it in between the other person and God, and does not condone it, how would you feel?

You may think that there is no justice if you forgive.

If you knew that forgiveness frees you from lugging round other people's failures but leaves justice to God, how would you feel?

———————— ● ————————

Forgiveness allows us to take back our power and freedom to focus on our best responses to life events. In no way do we deny what happened, the wrongdoings of other people, or the hurt that we have been through. We realize that we can shift the focus onto ourselves and our ability to make good choices, and we can let go of trying to control others. We can move past the hurt to a place of healthy boundaries, acceptance, and increased strength.

SELF-CARE

Love yourself for all you have been, all you are now, and all you have the power to become.[29]

Self-care is looking after one of God's kids, who happens to be you!

---

29. Karen Salmansohn.

Giving to and nurturing others is a very valuable thing, however, sometimes we may forget to give to and nurture one very important person: ourselves! We might be so busy extending ourselves to others that we forget ourselves in the process. This is not selfless, this is unhealthy!

You may think that self-care is a sweet extra rather than exactly what God wants of you.

If you knew that God wants you to take care of yourself, how would you view self-care?

———— ● ————

You may subconsciously doubt whether you are worthy of being taken care of.

If you knew that you are worth taking care of, what action would you take right now?

———— ● ————

You may disregard your needs and limitations as if you have no right to have them.

If you knew that you have a right to have needs and limitations, how would you feel?

———————— ● ————————

You may overlook the spiritual step of taking care of yourself and only view taking care of others as spiritual.

If you knew that taking care of yourself is a spiritual step, how would you view it differently?

———————— ● ————————

You may forget that you do not need to earn the right to receive attention and care.

If you knew that you deserve attention and care as God's child, how would that affect your decisions?

———————— ● ————————

When we acknowledge and respond to our own needs alongside giving to others, we do not end up resentful or burnt out. No one else can take responsibility for our self-care. Therefore, it is important that we commit to give ourselves the necessary physical, emotional, and spiritual up-keep that we need. We are worth being taken care of.

SELF-CRITICISM

You have been criticizing yourself for years and it hasn't worked. Try approving of yourself and see what happens.[30]

If your compassion does not include yourself, it is incomplete.[31]

Forgive yourself for not knowing what you didn't know before you learned it.[32]

---

30. Louise L. Hay.
31. Jack Kornfield.
32. Ann Silvers.

Because self-talk is invisible and happens internally, we may fail to see the huge impact it has on our lives. We may have an inner critic, a voice ready to pounce on us if we fail in any way. We subconsciously fear failure because of the harsh criticism that we subject ourselves to.

You may feel that only others are worthy of acceptance and compassion.

If you knew that you can give yourself the acceptance and compassion you would give others, what would you say to yourself?

———————— ● ————————

You may feel that you should be perfect and you need to treat yourself harshly if you ever make a mistake.

If you knew that it is OK to make mistakes, how would you feel?

———————— ● ————————

You may feel heroic for berating yourself for your shortcomings.

If you knew that God wants you to be on your own side, how would you feel?

———————— • ————————

You may judge your worth according to your performance, so if you fail, you feel like your worth plummets.

If you knew that you are unconditionally worthy, irrespective of performance, how would you feel?

———————— • ————————

You may feel that your failures and mistakes define you as a person, causing you to have a very low opinion of yourself.

If you knew that failures and mistakes are external of who you really are, how would you feel?

———————— • ————————

You may take your disempowering thoughts about yourself seriously and live your life under the influence of the resulting viewpoint.

If you knew that you do not need to take disempowering thoughts seriously, which thoughts would you let go of?

───────── ● ─────────

You may feel stuck and at the mercy of the conditions of worth you believe in, the "checklist" of what you have to prove to allow yourself to feel worthy.

If you knew that you have the capacity to let go of all your self-made conditions of worth and relax back into the knowledge of your unconditional worthiness, how would you feel?

───────── ● ─────────

The good news is that as disempowering as the inner critic is, when this voice changes to one of acceptance and compassion, it can be empowering. It can change our lives.

SELF-DOUBT

The day you were born is the
day God decided that the world
cannot exist without you.[33]

It's not who you are that holds you
back, it's who you think you are not.

Stop searching the world
for treasure; the real
treasure is in yourself.

---

33. Rabbi Nachman of Breslov.

We all have moments when we doubt ourselves. We doubt our ability and our value. The underlying assumption when we move into self-doubt is that we are not good enough and therefore cannot trust ourselves. We may be feeling insecure about a social situation, a decision we have made, or a relationship we are struggling with.

You may feel very limited in regard to the situations in life that you are dealing with.

If you knew that in this moment you are connected to infinite wisdom beyond the human mind, how would you feel?

———— • ————

You may feel stuck in the limited way of thinking you have been experiencing until now with regard to a certain situation.

If you knew that each moment offers a new opportunity to connect to the magnificent wisdom God is pouring through us, how would you feel?

You may focus on unimportant aspects of a situation or life in general, taking things personally rather than zoning in on the important things.

If you knew that you have the potential to gain perspective and zone in on what is important, what would you focus on?

You may feel insignificant and mistrust yourself to find solutions.

If you knew that you have tremendous power and wisdom within you how, how would you feel about yourself?

You may doubt your value.

If you knew that you are valued by God, how would you feel right now?

You may lose trust in yourself.

If you knew that you could trust yourself, how would you feel in the face of what you are dealing with?

———————— • ————————

You may feel the need to appear perfect in order to prove that you are enough.

If you knew that you are enough without needing to prove it, what would this realization give you?

———————— • ————————

You may doubt your value and significance.

If you knew that there is a specific role in this world that only you can fill, how would you see yourself?

———————— • ————————

You may feel that it is not OK that you have struggles, failures, or limitations.

If you knew that it is OK to have your individual blend of strengths and weaknesses, how would you feel?

———————— ● ————————

You may doubt your worthiness of receiving love.

If you knew that you are deserving of love, how would you feel?

———————— ● ————————

Whatever the circumstance we are dealing with, the good news is that when we connect to our inner acceptance and begin to trust ourselves as worthy spiritual beings who are constantly receiving a wellspring of wisdom and ability from God, our perspective shifts. Suddenly, we feel empowered in the face of whatever situation we are dealing with.

SOCIAL ANXIETY

If you find yourself constantly trying to prove your worth, you have already forgotten your value.

No one can make you feel inferior without your consent.[34]

---

34. Eleanor Roosevelt.

Social anxiety deserves a section of its own because it is such a common form of anxiety. We may dread social situations, worrying about appearing silly or incompetent. We may feel threatened. These fears are built on a foundational fear of not being good enough, which causes us to feel unimportant in relation to others and that we need to prove our worth.

You may feel that you have to change in order to be good enough.

If you knew that you are OK just the way you are, how would you feel right now?

———————— ● ————————

You may doubt that you are worthy and valuable.

If you knew that you are worthy and valuable, how would you feel right now?

———————— ● ————————

You may pressure yourself to feel comfortable instead of accepting that you feel self-conscious or unsure of yourself.

If you knew that you can stop judging yourself for feeling self-conscious and unsure of yourself and give yourself compassion and understanding, how would you feel?

———— • ————

You may feel stuck in your insecurity as long as you are in a particular social situation.

If you knew that your insecurity is coming from your mind, and your mind has the potential to shift, how would you feel?

———— • ————

You may feel the need for the approval of others to feel OK about yourself.

If you knew that you are a worthy person in your own right, what would this awareness give you?

———— • ————

You may feel that your lack of confidence has taken over your entire being.

If you knew that you have a confident place inside yourself, how would you feel?

—————— ● ——————

You may find yourself overanalyzing your social interactions.

If you knew that you do not have to overanalyze your social interactions, how would you feel?

—————— ● ——————

Learning to develop a supportive, compassionate relationship with ourselves paves the way for us to tackle social situations with a more solid grounding. Instead of fighting ourselves for struggling and feeling insecure, we can accept and reassure ourselves as we would do for someone we care about (that someone is us!).

WORRY

Worry does not take away tomorrow's troubles, it takes away today's peace.

Don't tell God how big your worries are, tell your worries how big God is.

We sometimes try to control aspects of our lives and the lives of others that are not in our hands. Deep down, we doubt that we (or others) are worthy of being taken care of by God and feel the need to desperately try to control life. We may doubt that we (or others) have the ability to cope. We may doubt our power. We may find ourselves constantly thinking about situations or people that we are worried about.

You may feel that it is essential that you worry about others.

If you knew that worry does not help the other person, it merely darkens your mind and heart, how would you feel about letting go of it?

———————— ● ————————

You may resist letting go of worry as you feel that doing so means you are letting go of caring.

If you knew that letting go of worry does not mean letting go of caring, how would you feel?

You may worry about things that you cannot control instead of focusing on the things that you can.

If you knew that you can let go of worrying about the future and focus on what you can control by taking responsible action in the moment, what would you do now?

———— ● ————

You may feel that you have to hold the people you care about in your mind all the time and that otherwise they will not be OK.

If you knew that you and everyone you care about are safely in God's hands, how would you feel?

———— ● ————

You may feel alone and unsupported.

If you knew that God is willing to partner with you in any area of your life if you reach out, what would you ask Him for?

———— ● ————

You may feel that you need to forge your own way through life.

If you knew that you are being carried by God through life, how would you feel?

———————— ● ————————

You may feel that you have been forgotten and there is no particular life direction for you.

If you knew that God has a clear path in life for you, how would you feel?

———————— ● ————————

You may feel that it is on your shoulders to save others from their difficulties.

If you knew that you need to do your best to help others but the results drop down directly from God how would your outlook change?

———————— ● ————————

You may find yourself overwhelmed thinking about
all the situations that need your attention.

**If you knew that all you need to focus
on right now is the purpose of this
moment, how would that help you?**

———————— ● ————————

Letting go of perceived control of our lives allows us to ease back into the awareness that
we are being taken care of by an all-loving,
all-knowing, all-powerful God who is imbuing us,
in every moment, with the resources we need
to deal with life. We are not letting go of anything real, only the mistaken assumption that
we need to carry ourselves through life. As a
result, we can wake up to the reality of being
carried.

ACKNOWLEDGMENTS

I am grateful to a number of people for enabling this book to come to fruition.

Each client I have had who have courageously and graciously shared their struggles, emotional blockages, and liberating triumphs with me. Each of you have contributed to the content of this book.

My family and friends who positively influence my life in numerous ways, particularly my enterprising and supportive husband who played a pivotal role in various aspects of the book.

Rabbi Moshe Kormornick of Adir Press, together with his dedicated staff have provided a high quality and swift service of editing and typesetting the manuscript which I am very grateful for.

My humble thanks go to God without Whom I would not be able to lift a finger let alone accomplish writing this book. My hope is that this book will help the reader to recognise the empowerment that they have in their lives and the value that He instils in them.

ABOUT THE AUTHOR

Deborah Saunders was born and educated in Manchester, England. She is a qualified therapist and runs a private practice in Manchester where she resides with her husband and children. She also runs popular workshops on emotional well-being, assertiveness, and parenting.

Deborah can be contacted via her website *www.finestmoments.org*

Printed in Poland
by Amazon Fulfillment
Poland Sp. z o.o., Wrocław